YOU KNOW
YOU'RE A
LIBRA
WHEN....

YOU KNOW YOU'RE A

WHEN....

100 RELATABLE FACTS ABOUT BEING A LIBRA

by Sarah Howell

....you can't make a decision without weighing all the options.

...you find harmony in the symmetry of things.

...your fashion sense is on point, and you're always dressed to impress.

...you're always the one mediating conflicts among friends.

....your home is filled with beautiful
art and decor.

...you're the go-to person for
relationship advice.

....you can't stand confrontations
and try to keep the peace.

...you're known for your charming
and diplomatic nature.

....you love social gatherings and can work a room like a pro.

...you're often accused of being a bit indecisive.

....you're a true romantic at heart.

...you're always striving for balance in your life.

...you're a natural peacemaker.

....you have a deep appreciation for art and culture.

...you're obsessed with symmetry and order.

....you love hosting dinner parties and gatherings.

...you're drawn to aesthetically pleasing environments.

...you can't resist a good debate or discussion.

YOU KNOW YOU'RE A LIBRA WHEN...

....you're constantly seeking fairness and justice.

...you're a natural charmer and can win people over easily.

...you have a knack for seeing both sides of an argument.

...you're a master of compromise.

...you appreciate the beauty in the little things.

....you're known for your tact and diplomacy.

...you enjoy indulging in the finer things in life.

...you're obsessed with keeping your social media feed aesthetically pleasing.

...you're a natural flirt without even trying.

....you believe in the power of love and partnership.

...you're constantly rearranging your furniture to find the perfect balance.

...you have a strong sense of justice and fairness.

...you can't resist buying beautiful jewelry.

...you're always striving for inner and outer beauty.

...you're a great listener and offer thoughtful advice.

...you're a sucker for a good love story.

...you're a natural diplomat and mediator.

...you find peace in nature and serene surroundings.

...you're drawn to careers in law, mediation, or counseling.

...you can't stand when things are out of balance or out of place.

...you're a die-hard fan of romantic comedies.

...you're known for your sense of style and fashion.

...you have a love for classical music and the arts.

...you're a natural at networking and building connections.

...you have a collection of scented candles to create a harmonious atmosphere.

...you can't resist a good spa day or self-care ritual.

...you're always striving to create a balanced diet and fitness routine.

...you appreciate the beauty of a handwritten letter or card.

...you're known for your impeccable manners.

...you enjoy the thrill of a good negotiation.

...you have a knack for making people feel valued and heard.

...you believe in the power of compromise in relationships.

...you're drawn to careers in design, fashion, or interior decorating.

...you can't resist a good spa day or massage.

...you have a playlist for every mood and occasion.

...you're always seeking harmony in your personal and professional life.

...you're known for your captivating smile.

YOU KNOW YOU'RE A LIBRA WHEN...

...you're a natural at giving compliments and making people feel special.

...you'd rather be single than settle for anything less than your ideal partner.

...you're a fan of aesthetically pleasing Instagram feeds.

... you're indecisive about your own birthday plans.

...you can't resist a beautiful sunset or sunrise.

...you're constantly torn between staying in for a cozy night or going out for a social event.

...you're drawn to careers in counseling, psychology, or therapy.

...you have a knack for creating a harmonious atmosphere in your home.

...you're a fan of romantic poetry and literature.

...you're known for your impeccable taste in wine and food.

...you have a talent for throwing elegant and memorable parties.

...you have a closet full of clothes but still can't find anything to wear.

...you're always seeking fairness and equity in the world.

...you can't resist a good spa retreat or weekend getaway.

...you have a deep love for all things beautiful and artistic.

...you're known for your ability to see both sides of an argument.

...you're a master of the art of seduction without even trying.

...you have a talent for arranging flowers and creating stunning bouquets.

...you can't resist rearranging your furniture every few weeks for that elusive sense of balance.

...you're drawn to careers in diplomacy, politics, or law.

...you can't make a decision without consulting your horoscope first.

...you're known for your ability to diffuse tension with your charm.

...you spend hours trying to find the perfect emoji to send in a text.

...you're a fan of beautiful landscapes and picturesque views.

...you have an innate ability to see the silver lining in every situation.

...you can effortlessly turn any mundane task into a creative endeavor.

...you have an uncanny knack for finding harmony in the most discordant of music.

...you believe that even the darkest of storms can reveal the most beautiful rainbows.

...you're a master of the art of compromise, even in the most challenging situations.

...your bookshelf is filled with a diverse range of titles, reflecting your ever-evolving interests.

...you're the one people turn to for advice on how to mend broken relationships.

...you have a special connection with animals and feel like you can communicate with them on a deeper level.

...you appreciate the beauty of handwritten letters and often pen heartfelt notes to loved ones.

...you can turn a simple meal into a culinary masterpiece with your presentation skills.

...you have a magnetic presence that draws people toward you like a moth to a flame.

...you believe that every person you meet has a unique story worth hearing.

...you're known for your impeccable taste in choosing the perfect gift for any occasion.

...you have a passion for collecting vintage items and uncovering the hidden stories behind them.

...you're a natural at hosting themed parties that transport guests to different eras and cultures.

...you can effortlessly bring opposing viewpoints together in a productive and harmonious discussion.

...you're drawn to professions that involve creative problem-solving and bridging gaps between people.

...you find beauty in the patterns of the stars and often contemplate the mysteries of the cosmos.

...you can turn a casual conversation into a deep philosophical exploration without missing a beat.

...you can make even the most mundane tasks feel like a meditation session.

...you find beauty in the way a single ray of sunlight dances through the leaves of a tree.

...you believe that every disagreement can be resolved with the right blend of empathy and compromise.

Milton Keynes UK
Ingram Content Group UK Ltd.
UKHW020808061023
430068UK00016B/731